SUPPLY AND DEMAND TRADING

Mastering- Trading zones and Trading strategies in Forex

Lewis wood

This book supply and demand trading is committed to each forex dealer and furthermore for fledgling brokers and amateurs who are keen on learning and trading the forex market including old merchants too with almost no experience, taking the necessary steps to win in forex trading, rather than giving reasons.

Introduction

Today, I will give you a full breakdown of how you can start trading the Supply and demand strategy.

With regards to exchanging the forex market, numerous brokers depend vigorously on specialized pointers and market opinion to recognize shifts in energy. Others, just exchange market lopsided characteristics via looking for organic market zones.

These zones are cost levels made by banks and foundations where unfilled orders are standing by to get filled. The entire idea of organic market is revolved around finding brilliant cash orders on a cost outline. Since they have the ability to move costs, they are the ones you ought to exchange with.

For you to exchange market lopsided characteristics, you really want to distinguish organic market zones accurately. That's what to do, there is a bunch of rules you need to keep to assist you with finding these zones on any resource you need to exchange. In this article, I will tell you bit by bit the best way to recognize organic market zones accurately on a cost diagram. I will likewise go through their various designs and show you live outline models toward the finish of the article.

Chapter 1

The crude powers of private enterprise rule markets like the laws of gravity. Purchasers and venders incite a fight to make a fair compromise understanding in each monetary market. As costs dance around on outlines, dealers are many times searching because of motivations to make sense of cost developments nonetheless, the hidden wellspring of cost development reduces to the connection among organic market.

By and large, positive news implies expanded request and decreased supply - likening to more exorbitant costs. Negative news generally spells lower interest and expanded supply.

This article will frame the accompanying primary parts of market interest:

What is supply and demand?
Supply and demand zones
Supply and demand in the forex market
How does supply and demand work?

WHAT IS SUPPLY AND DEMAND?

Supply and demand is the connection among purchasers and merchants that is utilized as an action for cost assurance in monetary business sectors. The powers of organic market interface to influence a balance cost among purchasers and dealers by which the amount of interest rises to the amount of supply.

What are the laws of supply and demand?

Supply' is absolutely the sum accessible, while 'request' is the sum that is wanted. The diagrams beneath demonstrate the visual part of supply, request and balance individually.

Supply: the connection among cost and amount

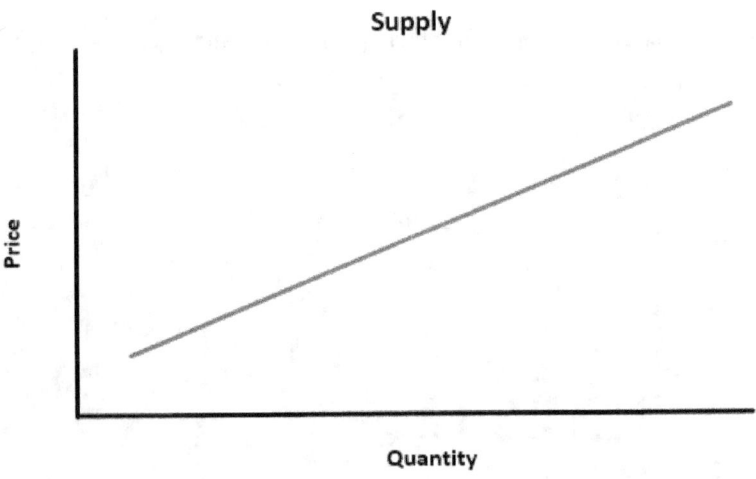

Demand: the relationship between price and quantity

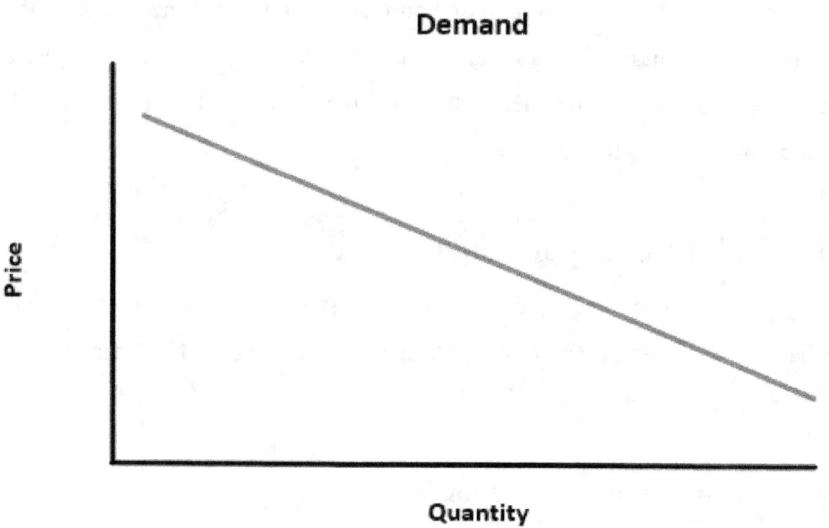

Demand

Price

Quantity

Equilibrium: the most efficient price at which quantity demanded equals the quantity supplied:

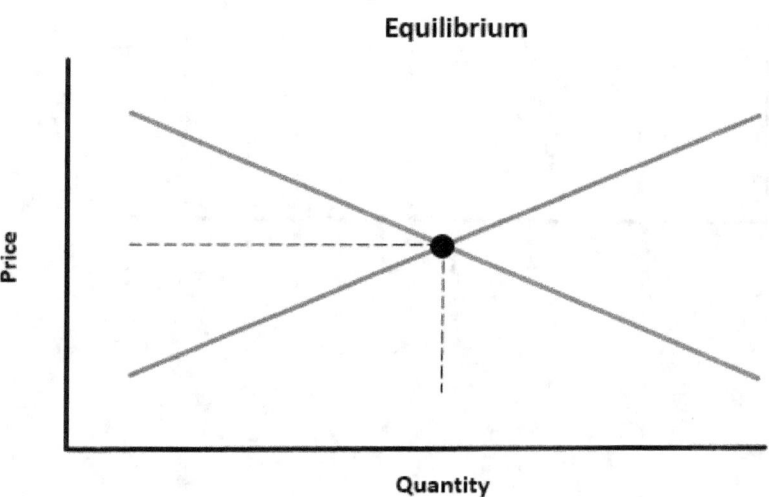

Equilibrium

Price

Quantity

SUPPLY AND DEMAND ZONES

Supply and demand zones permit merchants to acquire a discernment into the ongoing monetary business sectors, and these are outlined in the diagrams underneath.

It is observable that organic market zones cover a more extensive region rather than help and opposition levels. These more extensive zones give more dependable cost locales than a solitary line/level which can be a superior measure for future cost developments.

The supply zone beneath shows a region grouped by venders since value tends to 'bob' lower off this outlined zone. This fast cost development off these zones describes the elements of market interest zones. The interest zone shows similar qualities as the stock zone in the contradicting heading - request zone impersonates an expansive area of help.

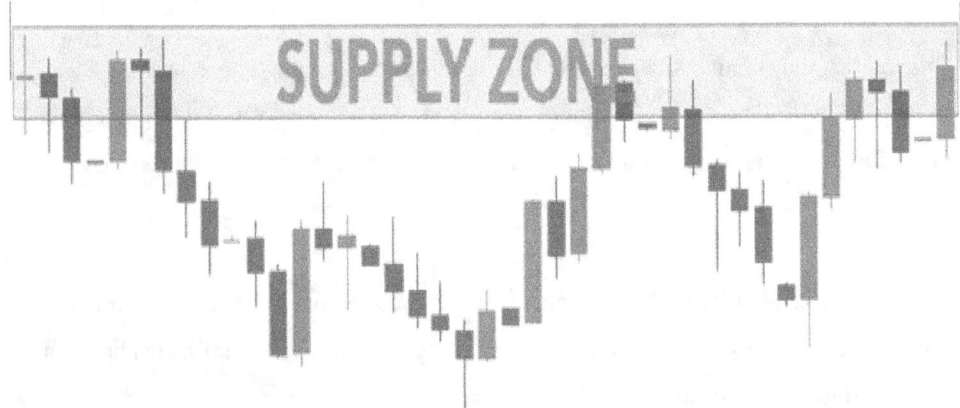

SUPPLY AND DEMAND IN THE FOREX MARKET

Supply and demand inside a straightforward vegetable market isn't quite unique from that which happens consistently in the forex market. At times, these powers are moving at such high speed that new dealers can experience issues grasping the granularity of the subtleties.

The forex market is the biggest monetary market on the planet in view of the weighty interest behind the exchanged resources. Monetary standards are the reason for the

world's economy and at whatever point one economy needs to exchange with another economy (gave various monetary forms are utilized) a trade will be required.

HOW DOES SUPPLY AND DEMAND WORK?

Basically, organic market works by investigating the amount of purchasers and dealers inside the forex market.

How in all actuality do market interest impact market cost?

Envision that the South African Hold Bank (SARB) institutes a financing cost change. A whole chain response will be gotten rolling because of the powers of organic market. At the point when rates increment, forex rollover installments additionally increment.

This implies that financial backers that are holding the exchange open at the predetermined rollover time (fluctuates from one country to another) will get a higher pace of interest than they would have beforehand - motivation has quite recently expanded.

All else being equivalent, more merchants would need to purchase; and less brokers would need to sell as the open door cost of selling (the rollover installment) has quite recently gotten more costly.

Chapter 2

Supply and demand forex – USD/ZAR daily chart:

Price attempting to find equilibrium with soaring ZAR demand

SARB increases rates

Demand escalates and price increases

As may be obvious, cost expects to find an agreeable point and will increment until there are no more purchasers able to follow through on that cost. As of now, venders dwarf purchasers, and cost will answer by dropping down.

After cost has dropped down sufficiently far (red circle) dealers will return into the image, recollecting in the expanded loan fee and the extra rollover installment that can be gotten from standing firm on a long ZAR situation, and this lower cost presents a 'apparent worth.'

As extra purchasers enter the image, cost will climb to mirror this expanded interest.

This is the course of value endeavoring to find its fair worth as it requires put on a wide range of investment outlines in each market on the planet.

USING SUPPLY AND DEMAND WITH SUPPORT AND RESISTANCE:

The connection among organic market alongside help and obstruction is significant. This is on the grounds that when cost crosses key help and obstruction levels, changes in organic market might happen inside that money pair.

Supply and demand are the actual determinants of cost - any cost. This applies to everything from your nearby ranchers market, to an intriguing, unique gem, to the unfamiliar trade market. Brokers that comprehend the elements of interest and supply are better prepared to comprehend current and future cost developments in the forex market.

This article covers the following talking points:

Supply and demand trading explained
Understanding Supply and Demand Zones
3 Tips for using supply and demand to trade forex
Supply and demand trading strategies

SUPPLY AND DEMAND TRADING EXPLAINED

Frequently, a money pair will move to an area of obstruction called a 'selling zone', where venders see there to be incredible selling potential at a generally overbought cost. The converse is likewise valid for money coordinates that drop to generally low levels, 'request zone' where purchasers see there to be extraordinary worth to purchase.

UNDERSTANDING SUPPLY AND DEMAND ZONES

Supply and demand zones are perceptible regions on a forex graph where cost has moved toward ordinarily previously. In contrast to lines of help and opposition, these look like zones more intently than exact lines.

Traders can customize charts to recognize the interest and supply zones as displayed on the USD/JPY beneath.

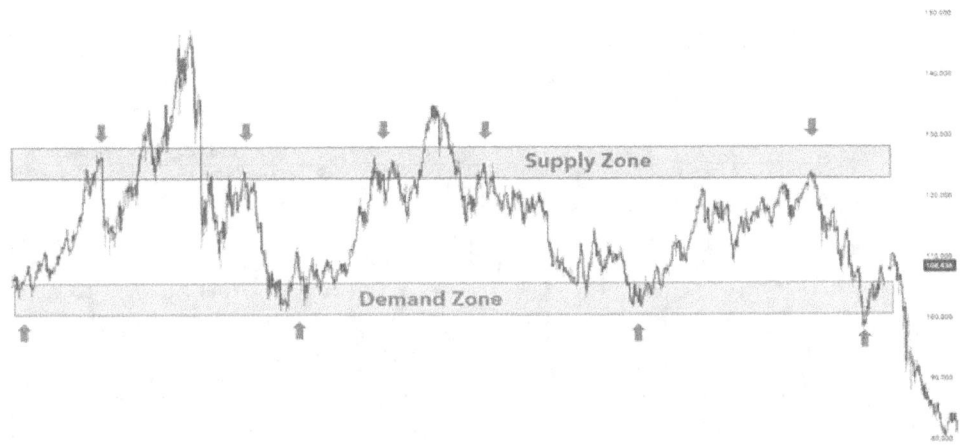

3 TIPS FOR USING SUPPLY AND DEMAND TO TRADE FOREX

1) Use longer time frames to identify supply and demand zones

By zooming out, brokers can get a superior perspective on regions where cost had skipped off beforehand. Make certain to utilize the fitting diagrams while changing the between numerous time spans. Attract a rectangular shape to mean this zone. Request and supply zones don't be guaranteed to need to show up together - frequently cash matches can uncover either.

2) Identify strong moves off the potential demand/supply zone

Certain cost levels offer worth to either bullish or negative brokers. When institutional merchants and large banks see this worth, they will hope to benefit from it. Subsequently, cost activity will in general speed up moderately rapidly until the worth has decreased or has been completely understood. Seeing different occasions of this at a similar cost level expands the likelihood that it is an area of significant worth and consequently, a stock or request zone.

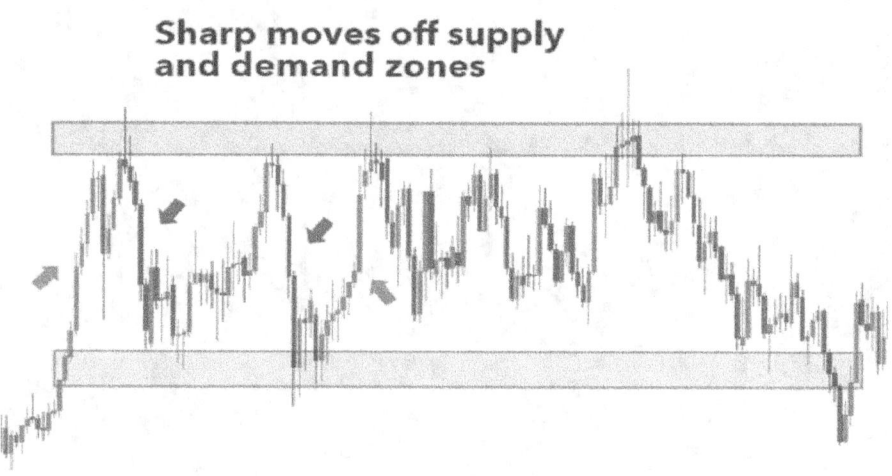

Sharp moves off supply and demand zones

3) Use pointers for affirmation of help and request zones

Traders can consolidate everyday or week by week turn focuses to distinguish or affirm supply or request zones. At Daily FX, we have a devoted page showing important help and obstruction levels for every significant market. Merchants ought to search for help and opposition levels to agree with request and supply zones for higher likelihood exchanges.

Moreover, traders can utilize Fibonacci levels for more prominent exactness on conceivable defining moments at supply or request zones. The 61.8% level is viewed as a huge level and compares with the stockpile zone in the outline beneath.

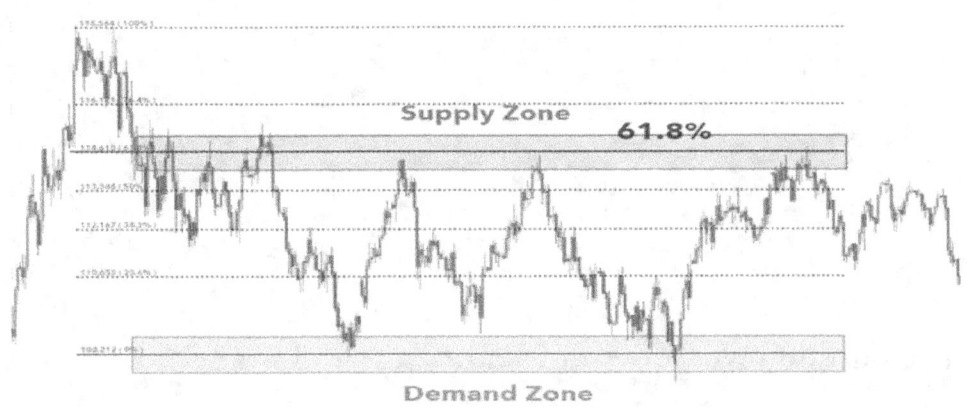

Chapter 3

SUPPLY AND DEMAND TRADING STRATEGIES

Range trading strategy

Supply and demand zones can be utilized for range exchanging in the event that the zones are deeply grounded. Dealers can consolidate the utilization of a stochastic pointer or RSI to help with distinguishing overbought and oversold conditions.

Since this is a non-directional exchange terms of the pattern, both long and short passages can be spotted. In the wake of survey oversold/overbought conditions on a more drawn out term diagram, dealers can zoom into a more modest time span to recognize an optimal passage.

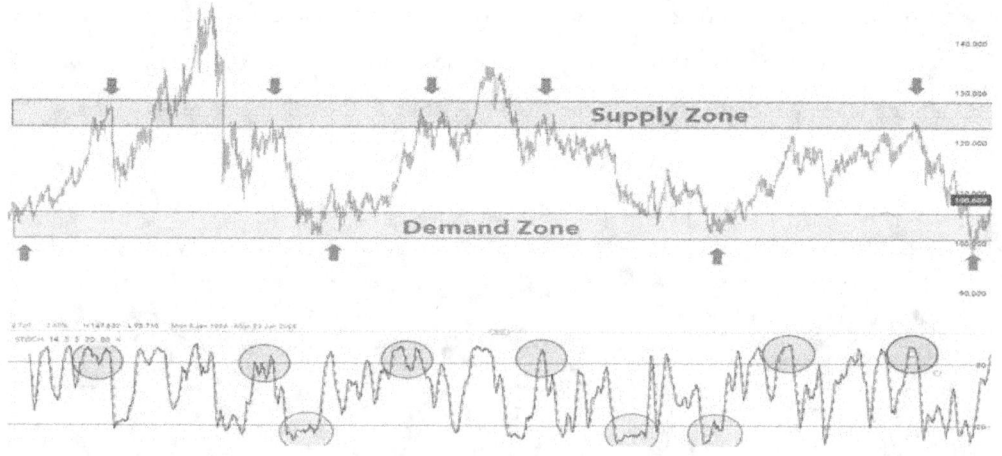

Breakout strategy

The breakout strategy is another supply and demand trading strategy. Cost can't stay inside a characterized range perpetually and will ultimately make a directional development. Brokers hope to acquire positive passage into the market, toward the breakout, as it could be the beginning of areas of strength for a.

The USD/JPY diagram shows a break of the exchanging range however at that point remembers back towards the interest zone. Merchants that place a short exchange at the breakout are helpless to being halted out in this situation. One method for relieving this is to expect the retracement back to the interest zone prior to pacing the short exchange.

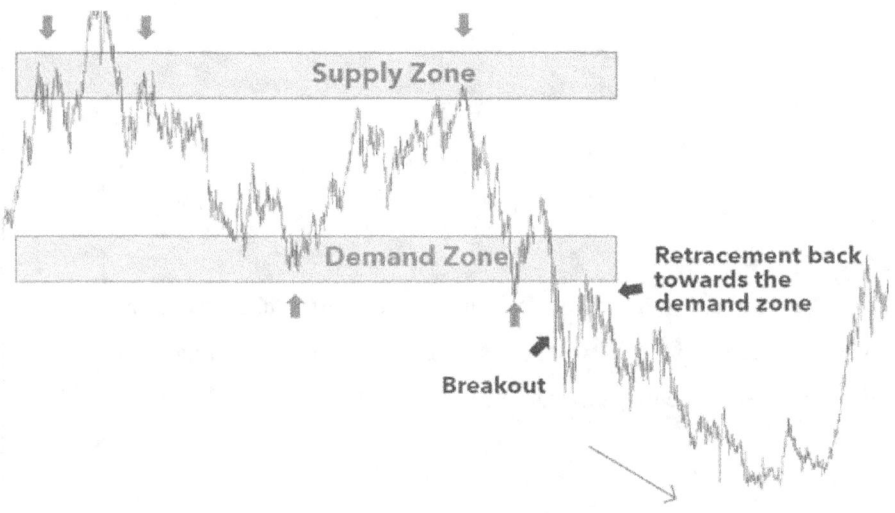

Using supply and demand zones as risk management parameters

Demand and supply zones are very similar to support and resistance and therefore, these areas provide an indication as to where a trader can place stops and limits.

These regions permit merchants to carry out a positive gamble to remunerate approach on all exchanges. Range merchants that are selling at the inventory zone can set stops over the stockpile zone and focuses at the interest zone. Moderate dealers can set the objective over the interest zone or execute various other gamble the board strategies.

The USD/SGD graph underneath demonstrates the way that stops and cutoff points can be put regarding supply and expectation zones:

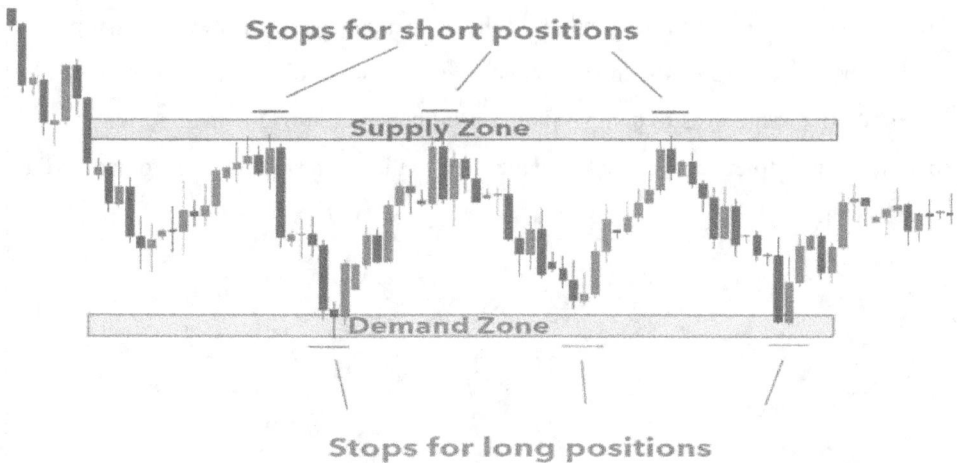

Supply and demand and support and resistance have a ton of likenesses, yet the point of this page is to recognize the two and distinguish how you can utilize backing and protection from exchange organic market.

THE DIFFERENCES BETWEEN SUPPLY AND DEMAND VS SUPPORT AND RESISTANCE:

Support and resistance are familiar with the concept of support and resistance, which is a level at which many unsuccessful attempts by price cannot be overcome. The supply and demand relationship consists of a much deeper zone that denotes broad support and resistance at key price levels.

SUPPLY AND DEMAND

Represented by a broad price region

Easier to find trade entries

SUPPORT AND RESISTANCE

Defined by a key price level

More difficult to base trade decisions

HOW TO USE SUPPORT AND RESISTANCE TO TRADE SUPPLY AND DEMAND

Trading Supply and Demand

The first thing traders need to do before placing a trade based on supply and demand is to decide whether the environment is expected to stay the same or to rapidly change. This can be evaluated by market instability estimates like huge political struggle or financial news. This is the division between the choice to exchange for a reach or exchange for a breakout.

Trading the Range

While exchanging a reach, merchants are expecting the climate to remain about something similar; with help or obstruction holding fast considering brokers to 'purchase low,' and 'sell high'. The diagram beneath outlines how a merchant can utilize cost alone to distinguish those focuses in the market at which request starts to overwhelm supply (making expanded costs) or supply starts to invade request (making diminished costs).

Trading the range with a GBP/USD chart

STRONG SELL POSITIONS

SELL WHEN PRICE TESTS RESISTANCE

BUY WHEN PRICE TESTS SUPPORT

STRONG BUY POSITIONS

Trading the Breakout

The opposite side of the coin is the merchant that is anticipating that the climate should change, with breaks of help or protection from make new highs or new lows.

With this style, the dealer's goal changes from the reach bound condition. The objective is presently to 'purchase high, and sell back at a greater cost,' or to 'sell low and repurchase to cover at a lower cost.'

Trading the breakout with a EUR/USD chart

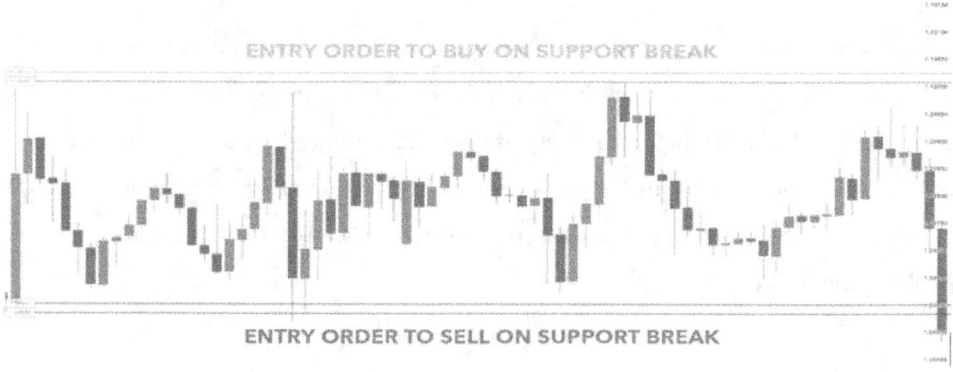

ENTRY ORDER TO BUY ON SUPPORT BREAK

ENTRY ORDER TO SELL ON SUPPORT BREAK

Chapter 4

Key levels in forex will more often than not cause to notice dealers on the lookout. These are mental costs which tie into the human mind and perspective. This article will cover the accompanying key regions about mental levels and round numbers in forex exchanging:

Psychological level definition

Identifying psychological levels

Using psychological levels to trade forex

Advantages and limitations of psychological levels

WHAT ARE PSYCHOLOGICAL LEVELS AND HOW DO THEY WORK?

Mental levels are market cost levels which are many times key levels in forex signified by round numbers. These round numbers much of the time go about as levels of help or potentially obstruction.

Mental help and obstruction reliably work due to principal human attitude. People esteem effortlessness; according to an exchanging point of view this implies esteeming entire numbers. Merchants frequently utilize these numbers as passage, exit or stop levels. These stops and cutoff points can adjust request stream and cost changes.

IDENTIFYING PSYCHOLOGICAL LEVELS ON FOREX CHARTS

Brokers will frequently call these entire number spans 'twofold zeros,' as these costs are at even numbers, for example, 1.31000 on EUR/USD, 1.57000 on GBP/USD or 132.00 on GBP/JPY. The outline beneath distinguishes the 'twofold zeros' on the ongoing USD/JPY diagram.

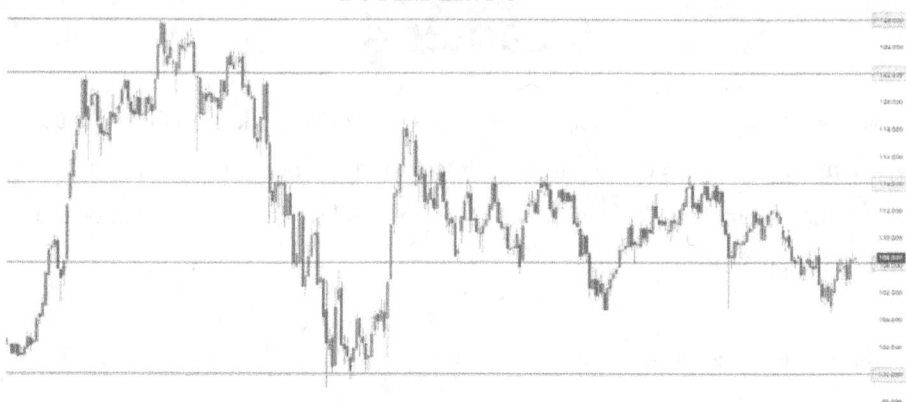

Some traders will make this a stride further by taking a gander at the number straightforwardly in the center of these entire numbers or 'the fifties.' These levels, for example, 1.31500 on EUR/USD or 131.50 on GBP/JPY can frequently become possibly the most important factor in similar way as the 'twofold zeros.'

Brokers will see that there will frequently be some component of clog at these vital levels in forex as costs go up or down. The outline underneath delineates USD/ZAR with 'fifties' indicated.

Notice that a considerable lot of the cost swings on the above graph occur around one of these levels. Consequently, merchants need to integrate these levels into the help and opposition updates. The graph beneath addresses the underlying USD/JPY outline with distinguished swing levels.

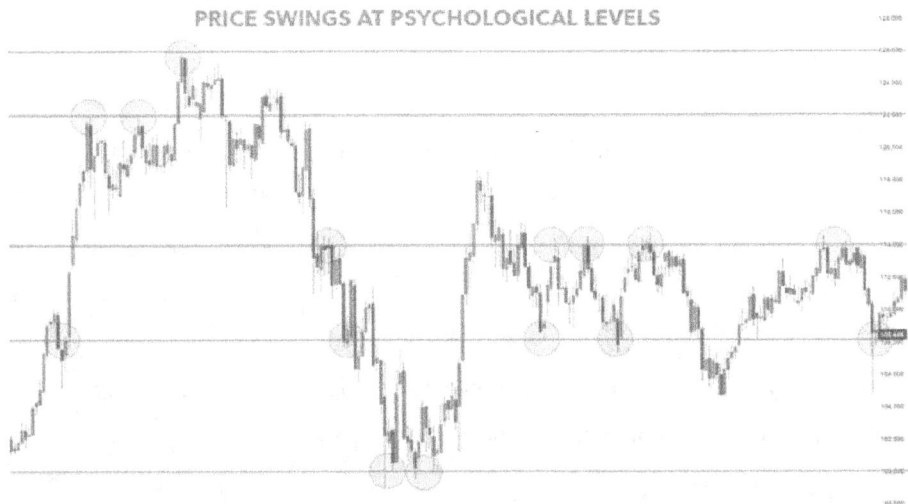

PRICE SWINGS AT PSYCHOLOGICAL LEVELS

Thus, these costs go about as a mental line which function admirably as help and opposition. Few out of every odd one of these costs go about as an element of help or opposition, however enough do that these levels warrant the merchant's consideration.

HOW TO USE PSYCHOLOGICAL LEVELS IN FOREX TRADING
AUD/JPY weekly chart

INFLECTION POINTS

On the AUD/JPY outline above there are major areas of strength for six off the 75.00 cost level. Each time cost moved toward 75.00, the cash pair returned quickly up. This is on the grounds that:

Dealers saw the cost of 75.00 and accepted this is modest which incited long AUD compromises this level.

As dealers were opening short positions, benefit targets were set at an even 75.00. This benefit target request to close positions provoked interest on the lookout (brokers were purchasing to cover, and this purchasing interest is considered 'request').

After the primary emphasis, dealers might not have been incredibly bullish on the possibility of pushing cost a lot of lower than 75.000 as this cost has proactively been displayed as help.

In numerous ways, untested 'mental' levels can be seen like turn focuses. A region where there perhaps some component of help or obstruction.

As a rule, round numbers, for example, 70.000 on AUD/JPY or 1.0000 on AUD/USD will earn more consideration than a more common level like 71.000 on AUD/JPY. Most merchants will frequently dole out a more significant level of solidarity to the more adjusted stretches.

Where merchants can truly find esteem with these levels is when costs might have opposed or been upheld there previously. This lets the merchant know that others are seeing and following up on those costs, and the potential for the 'unavoidable outcome' of specialized investigation may possibly be considered with more strength.

ADVANTAGES AND LIMITATIONS OF PSYCHOLOGICAL LEVELS

Key levels in forex ought to be evaluated in accordance with the latest thing and whether there is optional specialized ideas for the exchange. The following are the benefits and impediments of mental levels:

ADVANTAGES

Serves as key levels of support and resistance

Easy to identify for novice traders

LIMITATIONS

Not always 100% reliable as a key level

Should be used as a guideline in conjunction with supporting indicators/technical analysis techniques.

A forex pivot point technique could in all likelihood be a dealer's dearest companion similarly as recognizing levels to foster a predisposition, place pauses and distinguish potential benefit focuses for an exchange.

Pivot points have been a go-to for dealers for quite a long time. The premise of turn focuses is to such an extent that cost will frequently move comparative with a past breaking point, and except if an external power makes the cost do as such, cost ought to stop close to an earlier limit. Turn point exchanging techniques change which makes it a flexible instrument for forex brokers.

Defining the pivot point

How to calculate pivot points

Using pivot points in forex trading

Pivot point trading strategies

Difference between pivot points and Fibonacci retracements

Chapter 5

WHAT IS A PIVOT POINT?

A pivot point is a is a technical indicator used by forex traders as a price level gauge for potential future market movements. The pivot point indicator is used to determine trend bias as well as levels of support and resistance, which in turn can be used as profit targets, stop losses, entries and exits.

Pivot point example:

PIVOT POINT

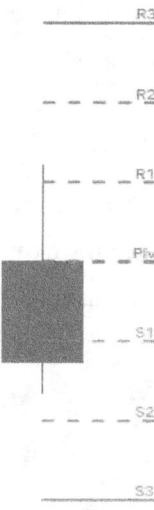

HOW TO CALCULATE PIVOT POINTS

The calculation for the most basic flavor of pivot points, known as 'floor-trader pivots,' along with their support and resistance levels:

Pivot point formula

Pivot point (PP) = (High + Low + Close) / 3

First resistance (R1) = (2 x PP) – Low

First support (S1) = (2 x PP) – High

Second resistance (R2) = PP + (High – Low)

Second support (S2) = PP – (High – Low)

Third resistance (R3) = High + 2 (PP – Low)

Third support (S3) = Low – 2 (High – PP)

There are other ways to calculate the pivot point, which is accessible on most exchanging stages and can be stretched out through various time spans. The help and obstruction levels will be determined as above. The following is an illustration of what is presented on the IG exchanging stage for everyday turns. A similar computation can be made for week by week or month to month turns as well:

How did the pivot point calculation come about?

As of not long ago, PCs were not accessible on a mass scale. Thusly, market creators and floor merchants required an approach to deciding if cost was 'modest' or 'costly' on a relative premise. From a basic numerical computation, turn focuses were conceived.

Dealers basically took the high, low, and shutting cost from the past time frame and partitioned by three to track down the 'turn.' From this turn, merchants would then base their estimations for three help, and three obstruction levels.

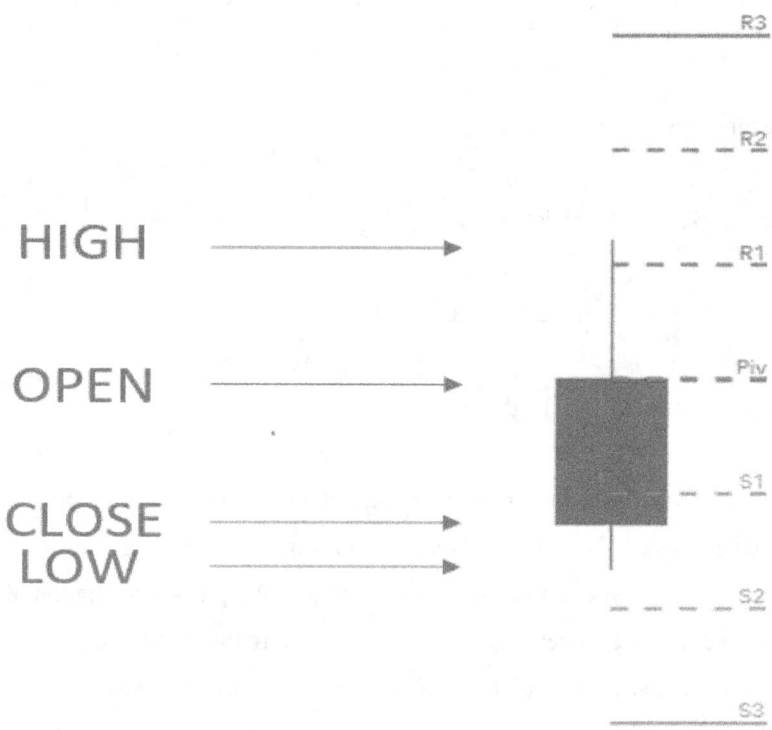

HOW TO USE PIVOT POINTS IN FOREX TRADING

Turn focuses are involved by forex merchants in accordance with conventional help and obstruction exchanging strategies. Value will in general regard these levels as they do with help and obstruction. Turn point cost levels are repetitively tried which further validates these levels.

Brokers every now and again utilize extra approval devices, for example, pointers, candle designs, oscillators, basics and value activity to use related to the turn to settle on exchange choices the forex market.

There are a couple of fundamental rules to keep while exchanging with turn focuses:

Price above pivot = bullish bias

Price below pivot = bearish bias

Longer period turn directs are more trustworthy due toward expanded informational index

Backing and obstruction levels are expansions of the turn which can be utilized as strengthening key cost levels

Turn POINT Exchanging Methodologies

1. Turn point swing exchanging

For merchants who favor the medium to longer-term exchanges, swing exchanging with the turn point is conceivable by utilizing week after week/month to month time periods.

The outline underneath portrays a week by week graph with the expansion of the turn point no one but (this can be altered by changing the turn settings on the stage). It is clear there has been a pattern inversion to the potential gain which is obvious after the cost gets through the past turn obstruction.

Presently going about as a help level, forex brokers can put in lengthy passage requests at the turn cost. There is a bogus breakout (blue circle) yet after this, there is significant potential gain which could be taken advantage of. The turn levels will not necessarily contain the cost, however it offers a value level to keep up with the directional inclination. This would be a lengthier time skyline which would be great for swing dealers.

USD/ZAR weekly chart

FALSE BREAKOUT

PIVOT ACTING AS SUPPORT,
BUY ENTRY ORDERS AT PIVOT

2. Turn point breakout procedure

Numerous dealers endeavor to concentrate their exchanging action to the more unpredictable periods the market when the potential for huge moves might be raised.

Dealers might endeavor to take a gander at breaks of each help or obstruction level as a chance to enter an exchange a quick market. This can be especially significant for longer-term turn levels, with center being paid to the week after week and month to month turn focuses. The outlines underneath will demonstrate the way that a merchant can set up a turn point breakout procedure utilizing first and foremost the turn alone as a sign as well as the more mind boggling help and obstruction levels.

The outline underneath shows a turn point with help and obstruction levels prohibited. In this model, the turn marker is based over a week after week time frame which furnishes merchants with a lengthy informational index for a more dependable key level. The turn is utilized as a key cost level, which was at first regarded a couple of candles before the breakout. When the breakout happens, dealers can then hope to go into a long exchange as cost over the turn flags a bullish inclination.

USD/ZAR four-hour chart

Floor-Trader Pivots help brokers in recognizing regions in a graph where cost is probably going to approach and can be utilized to set suitable focuses, while really overseeing risk. It is one of many sorts of turn focuses brokers can use to decide key levels, however the idea of help and opposition is very much settled in every one of them.

Keep reading to learn more about:

Definition of Floor-Trader Pivots
How to calculate Floor-Trader Pivots
Trading with Floor-Trader Pivots

Chapter 6

WHAT ARE FLOOR Merchant Turns?

Floor-Trader Pivots, also known as 'Classical Pivots', mean regions on a graph where future cost is probably going to experience backing or opposition. The turn focuses are determined by a particular recipe that considers past value information; and tasks three degrees of help and obstruction based around the 'turn' itself.

The name 'Floor-Dealer Turns' comes from a period before internet exchanging where 'floor broker's required a simple recipe to decide if a cost was moderately modest or costly prior to yelling offers and offers across the room.

Advanced merchants hoping to copy the floor dealers can do as such effortlessly as most graphing bundles have turn focuses remembered for the determination of pointers.

HOW TO CALCULATE FLOOR TRADER PIVOTS

The default time frames include daily, weekly or monthly pivot points and they can be calculated as follows:

The Pivot: (Previous high + previous low + previous close) / 3

PIVOT LOCATION RELATIVE TO PRICE
Price above pivot
Price below pivot

DIRECTION BIAS
Bullish bias
Bearish bias

R1: (Current pivot Value X 2) – Previous Low

R2: Current pivot + (R1 – S1)

R3: Current pivot – (R2 – S2)

S1: (Current pivot value X 2) – Previous High

S2: Current pivot value – (R1 – S1)

S3: Current pivot value – (R2 - S2)

Many traders scour the web looking for Floor-Merchant Turn mini-computers to ascertain the qualities for each market of revenue. Daily FX eliminates this problem with our devoted page on turn focuses; illustrating R1, R2, R3, turn, S1, S2, S3 for every single top market. The page can be custom fitted to show hourly, day to day, week after week and month to month information and can be applied to Traditional, Camarilla and Woodie Turns.

USING FLOOR-TRADER PIVOTS: TOP TIPS

1. Filter trades in the direction of the trend

In deep rooted downtrends, there are more pips to profit from toward the pattern rather than pips on offer against the pattern. Dealers can utilize the help and obstruction focuses to search for breakout exchanges the bearing of the pattern. The idea is straightforward, albeit the graph can be fairly jumbled.

As you can find in the graph underneath (featured in blue), the S1 and S2 groups go about as obstruction focuses in the current downtrend. Forex brokers will hope to submit passage requests a couple of pips beneath these levels to catch further disadvantage developments in cost.

NZD/USD daily chart:

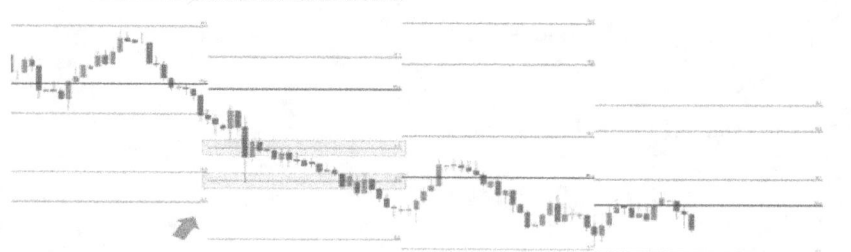

2. Floor-Trader Pivots present attractive entries

Old style turns can introduce appealing sections while exchanging the course of the pattern. The graph underneath zooms into a current downtrend, showing how cost backtracks up towards the turn prior to going on down. Merchants can set working requests at these levels or basically enter short after cost has arrived at the turn and dropped down.

GBP/USD daily chart:

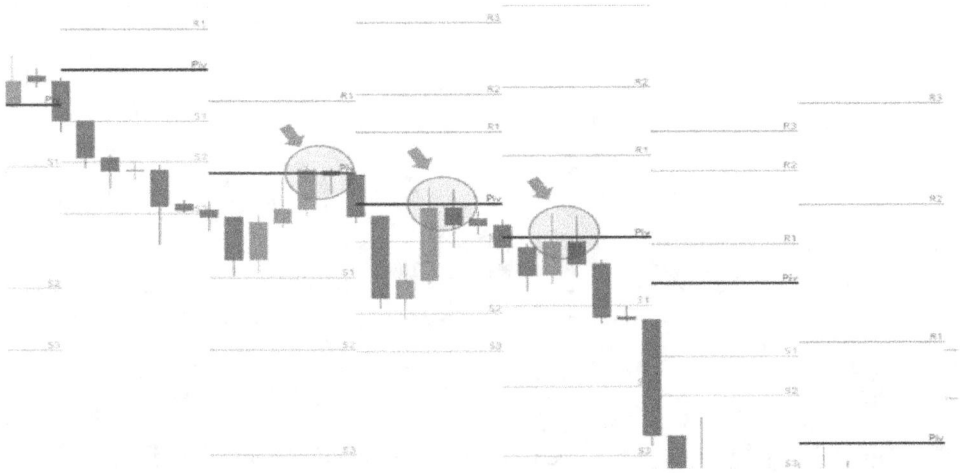

3. Using Floor-Trader Pivots as dynamic support and resistance

Traders can use the levels of support provided by the Floor-Trader Pivots as dynamic support or dynamic stops.

This turns out to be clear while noticing the underneath GBP/USD graph beneath. As cost climbs, the S1 level climbs as well and merchants can trail their stops in accordance with this level to secure in benefits in the event that the market turns around. More tight stops will trail the S1 in an upswing and stops set at the S2 and S3 can be utilized in additional unstable business sectors gave a more modest exchange size is used.

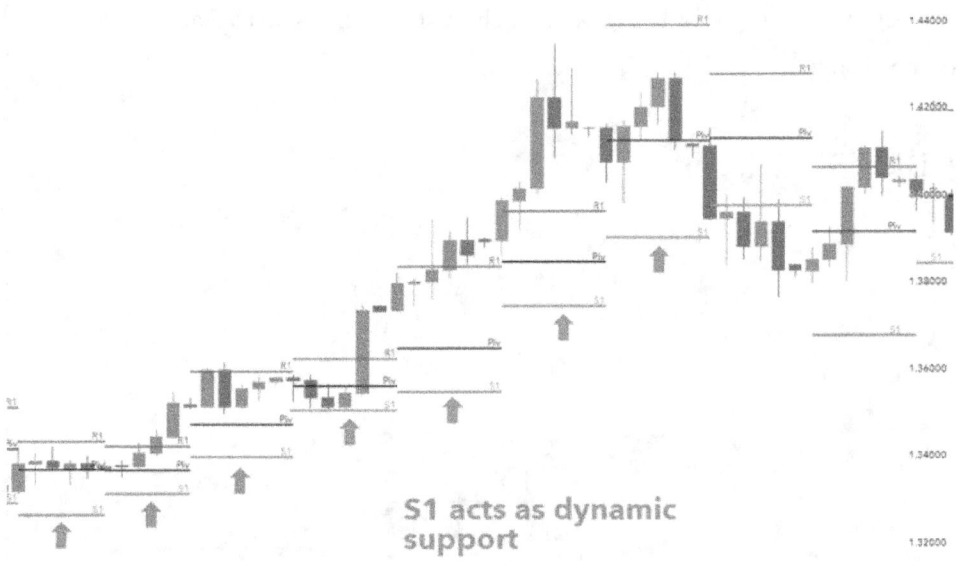

S1 acts as dynamic support

The Camarilla turn direct is a flexible pointer that permits brokers toward perceive key cost levels, section focuses, leave focuses and fitting gamble the executives. The best Camarilla turn exchanging technique is subject to the economic situations at a given time. These economic situations will direct the most proper Camarilla technique to utilize. There are different Camarilla turn direct systems toward exchange any monetary market. This article will cover the accompanying primary ideas:

Definition of a Camarilla pivot point
Camarilla trading strategies
Advantages and limitations of trading with camarilla pivot points

Chapter 7

WHAT IS A CAMARILLA PIVOT POINT?

A Camarilla turn point is an expansion of the traditional/floor merchant turn point which gives dealers key help and obstruction levels. There are four help and four opposition levels remembered for the Camarilla turn, as well as extensively closer levels than other turn varieties - see picture underneath. This closeness makes the Camarilla ideal for momentary merchants.

Proximity of Camarilla pivot points vs Classic pivot points

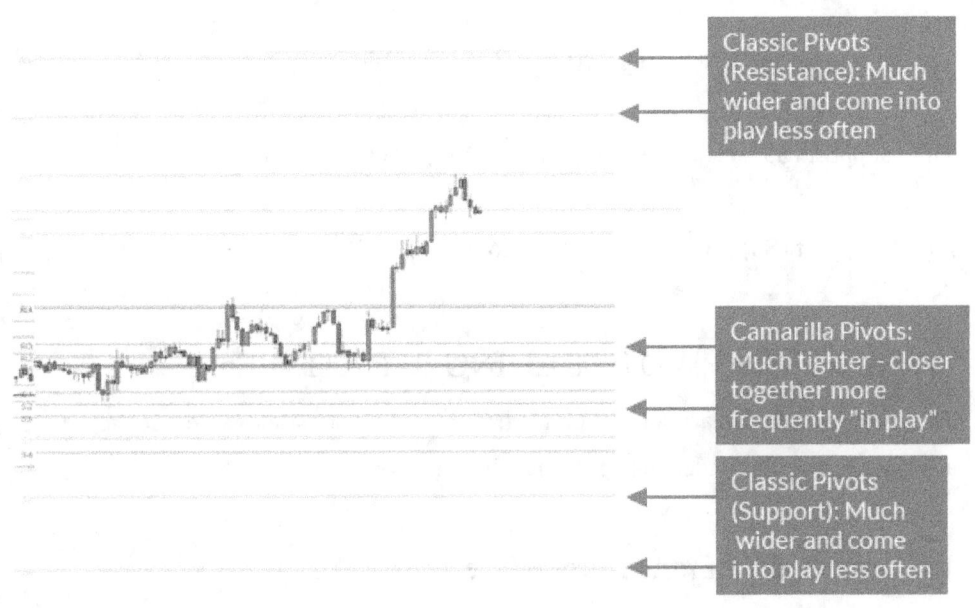

Follow our hourly, daily, weekly and monthly Camarilla pivot points through our Daily FX pivot page pivot pointsto determine market sentiment.

CAMARILLA EQUATION FORMULA

The calculation for Camarilla pivot points along with its support and resistance levels:

Fourth resistance (R4) = Closing + ((High -Low) x 1.5000)

Third resistance (R3) = Closing + ((High -Low) x 1.2500)

Second resistance (R2) = Closing + ((High -Low) x 1.1666)

First resistance (R1) = Closing + ((High -Low x 1.0833)

Pivot point (PP) = (High + Low + Closing) / 3

First support (S1) = Closing – ((High -Low) x 1.0833)

Second support (S2) = Closing – ((High -Low) x 1.1666)

Third support (S3) = Closing – ((High -Low) x 1.2500)

Fourth support (S4) = Closing – ((High-Low) x 1.5000)

CAMARILLA PIVOT TRADING STRATEGIES

There are several Camarilla pivot point strategy techniques. Below are three favored approaches used by traders using this handy indicator.

1) Camarilla turn range procedure

A reach is known as a sideways market with cost exchanging between laid out lines of help and obstruction. Range merchants can benefit extraordinarily from Camarilla turns, as every day the pointer will offer another reach for exchanging. As seen underneath brokers searching for transient reach inversions ought to fundamentally zero in on cost moving between the S3 and R3 turns. This region is known as the

everyday exchanging range and can permit range brokers clear regions to design their market passages.

Generally, range inversion merchants will search for cost to push toward either a mark of help or obstruction. Assuming opposition holds range dealers will hope to start short situations close to the R3 turn, with the purpose of value moving to help. On the other hand, assuming that cost stays upheld over the S3 Camarilla turn, range merchants will hope to start purchase based positions close to the S3 turn with the goal of cost moving back towards the R3 obstruction turn. In any case, it ought to be noticed that cost can remain range bound over the course of the day.

This procedure works best in low unpredictability periods like the Asian exchanging meeting. In additional unstable times, brokers will hope to get away from this system to something more comprehensive of sporadic cost developments - see technique 2 underneath.

Typical Camarilla pivot setup

2) Camarilla turn pattern methodology

A trend is areas of strength for a move that pushes cost either sequential over a predetermined time frame. The Camarilla turn can be incredibly valuable during moving business sectors, and furnish dealers with key passage, pause and cutoff levels. Brokers will hope to channel sections toward the pattern. On the off chance that the market is moving up, search for purchasing open doors at the S3, stop at S4. Assuming that the market is moving down, sell R3 and stop at R4.

The diagram beneath shows an AUD/JPY outline in an upswing. In view of this, brokers will be searching for long sections at S3 with stops at S4 as shown. There are different techniques to recognize take benefit levels like Fibonacci augmentations/retracements, cost activity or other specialized pointers. This choice is at the carefulness of the singular broker.

ADVANTAGES AND LIMITATIONS OF TRADING WITH CAMARILLA PIVOT POINTS

DVANTAGES OF CAMARILLA PIVOT POINTS

1. Beneficial for short-term traders
2. Improves traders risk management
3. Works well in all financial markets

LIMITATIONS OF CAMARILLA PIVOT POINTS

1. May not be ideal for longer-term traders
2. Can be difficult to implement for novice traders
3. Applying the wrong strategy to the wrong market condition can lead to additional losses

RELATIVE STRENGTH INDEX – TALKING POINTS:

What is Relative Strength Index (RSI)?

How do you calculate Relative Strength Index?

What does the Relative Strength Index tell you?

Relative Strength Index: A Summary

Become a Better Trader with Our Trading Tips

WHAT IS RELATIVE STRENGTH INDEX (RSI)?

The Relative Strength Index (RSI) is a specialized examination device that is utilized to gauge the level of late value development of a resource/market to decide overbought or oversold conditions. The RSI is alluded to as a force oscillator which vacillates somewhere in the range of 0 and 100.

Notice the 'mid-line' at 50 in the picture underneath - brokers will oftentimes involve this as a cut-off. In the event that the RSI is perusing over 50, dealers will believe the pattern to be bullish. In the event that RSI is under 50, dealers will frequently believe the force to be negative. Merchants have likewise made this a stride further, with the possibility that in the event that RSI goes north of 70 - the pair isn't just bullish, yet possibly overbought. On the other hand, brokers frequently expect to be that in the event that RSI is under 30 - the pair isn't simply negative, it very well might be oversold.

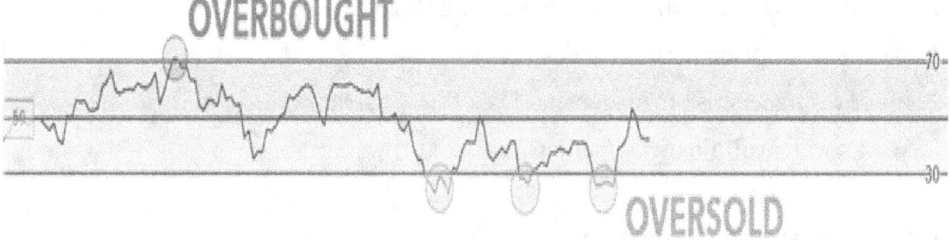

HOW DO YOU CALCULATE RELATIVE STRENGTH INDEX?

Relative Strength Index (RSI) is calculated by:

relative strength index (RSI) formula

RSI was created by specialist, mathematician, and merchant J. Welles More stunning. More stunning was a stock and items dealer at that point and he experienced a typical issue with respect to timing of exchange passage and leave focuses. More stunning then fostered an equation to beat this test and permit brokers to more readily time long and short section/leave focuses.

RSI will grade the cost development displayed between candles for the last 'X' time frames (with 'X' being the info utilized by the dealer, normally 14 with RSI). As cost changes, RSI will enlist these progressions in cost - comparative with past value developments to show market 'strength.'

WHAT DOES THE RELATIVE STRENGTH INDEX TELL YOU?

There are multiple ways of involving the RSI in exchanging, which will be illustrated in the models underneath:

The initial two pictures underneath address the most essential technique for utilizing the RSI by deciphering overbought and oversold crossroads by which potential exchange passage focuses happen.

1. Overbought signal USD/ZAR - The USD/ZAR outline shows an overbought RSI signal over the '70' level demonstrating potential short section open doors.

2. Oversold signal GBP/USD - The GBP/USD chart shows an oversold RSI signal below the '30' level indicating potential long entry opportunities.

Dissimilarity is one more significant method for utilizing the RSI marker. Difference is an instrument used to recognize possible inversions by looking at the development among pointer and market course. The diagrams beneath represent positive (bullish inversion) and negative (negative inversion) difference signals.

3. Positive disparity USD/JPY - The USD/JPY diagram shows falling costs alongside rising RSI levels flagging an inversion in pattern to the potential gain.

4. Negative difference USD/JPY - The USD/JPY graph displays rising costs alongside falling RSI levels flagging an inversion in pattern to the drawback.

Conclusion

In summary supply and demand analysis is the fundamental device of microeconomics and has become the foundation of a market economy. The laws of supply and demand aimis to make sure that the market always re calibrates to balance. As in serious business sectors, supply and demand bends decide the sum created by firms and request by purchasers as a function of cost. A few variables assume the part in influencing request and supply in different positive and negative ways. The demand curve shows the connection between the cost of an item and the amount of the item requested. The factors that influence the interest bend are changes intastes and inclinations, pay level, cost of substitute, supplements, assumption for future price, and changes in purchaser socioeconomic. Interestingly, the supply curve shows the relationship between the cost of an item and the quantity of the items provided. The factors that influence